The Buildings
of Warwick

1 The interior of Beauchamp Chapel

The Buildings of Warwick

RICHARD K. MORRISS

With photographs by Ken Hoverd

ALAN SUTTON PUBLISHING LIMITED

First published in the United Kingdom in 1994
Alan Sutton Publishing Limited
Phoenix Mill · Far Thrupp · Stroud · Gloucestershire

First published in the United States of America in 1994
Alan Sutton Publishing Inc. · 83 Washington Street · Dover
NH 03820

British Library Cataloguing-in-Publication Data

ISBN 0–7509–0558–1

A catalogue record for this book is available from the British
Library

Library of Congress Cataloging-in-Publication Data applied for

Cover illustrations: *front*: The ornate 'timber framing' of the
Master's House in Lord Leycester's Hospital is in fact a
nineteenth-century wall plastered and painted to look like the
original; *front inset*: St Peter's chapel sits astride the East Gate;
back: One of the many classic views of Warwick Castle –
arguably one of the finest in Europe.

Typeset in 11/14 Times.
Typesetting and origination by
Alan Sutton Publishing Limited.
Printed in Great Britain by
Ebenezer Baylis, Worcester.

Contents

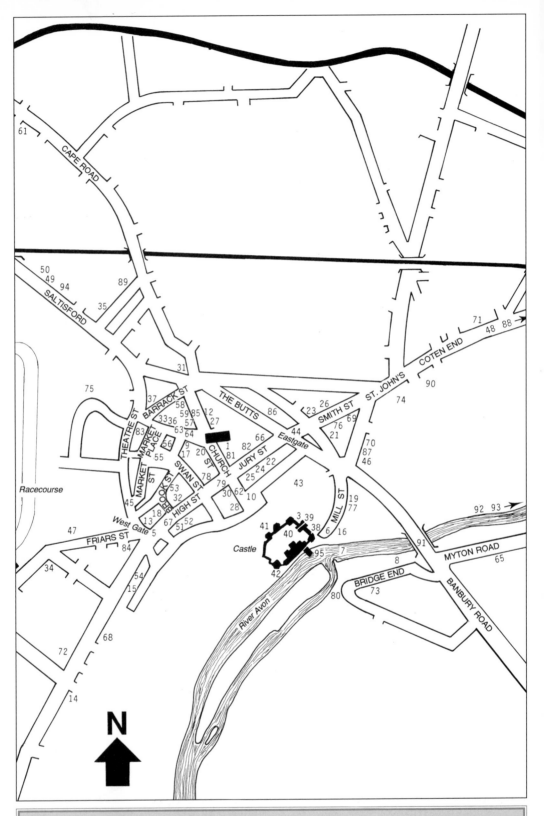

N

Warwick. The numbers on the map refer to building numbers in the captions

Introduction

*The towne of Warwike stondithe on a mayne rokky hille,
risynge from est to west. The beawty and glory of the towne
is 2 strets, whereof the one is caullyd the Highe Strete and
goith from the est gate to the west, having a right goodly
crosse in the middle of it. The other crossith the midle of it,
makynge Quadrivium and goith from northe to southe.*

John Leland, *c.* 1535

Historic Warwick, county town of leafy Warwickshire, lies at
the very heart of England. It is, then, perhaps strange to realize
that the town was only established here as one of a line of
border strongholds to guard the emerging English nation from
the invading Danes. Before this there was probably a small
Saxon settlement by the natural weir across the Avon, and at
the very north-eastern tip of the kingdom of the *Hwicce*, later
part of Mercia. Its early name, *Waerinc Wicum*, recorded on a
deed of 1001, simply meant 'a settlement by a weir'. Then, in
914 AD, Aethelflaeda, Lady of the Mercians, sister of Edward
the Elder and daughter of the great King Alfred, chose the site
as one of her ten new *burhs*.

Warwick possessed few advantages. It was not a natural route
centre; the Avon was too small for regular navigation; and the
nearest Roman road, the Fosse Way, bypassed the town several
miles to the east. This in turn meant it was not a natural market
or an administrative centre – but none of this mattered to
Aethelflaeda. What Warwick did have was the best defensive
site in the area – a rocky bluff overlooking the weir – and it was
on top of this that Aethelflaeda established the new settlement.
The *burh* was part of a line of strongholds designed to offer

safety to the locals in time of war and to be a constant threat to the Danes occupying the region to the north-east.

The natural defences of the new town were probably strengthened by a ditch and rampart around the high ground, though tantalizingly few traces of Saxon Warwick have come to light. It is possible that the later medieval defences followed those of the tenth century. Aethelflaeda and Edward's campaigns against the Danes were successful and Warwick itself benefited. It was made the county town of a new, and rather artifically created, *scire* – Warwickshire – formed by joining what had been northern *Hwicce* with some Mercian territory. As a result, it also became a market centre, was given its own mint, and, by the time of the Norman conquest, was a thriving town. The Domesday Book, produced in 1086, twenty years after the conquest, recorded at least 248 houses in Warwick – suggesting a sizeable population for the period, approaching 2,000.

The late-Saxon town of *Waerincwican* seems to have had a very simple layout, with four streets meeting in the middle of the town, three leading to the west, north and east gates in the defences, and the fourth going down to the river crossing to the south. Other streets followed the line of the defensive ditch, inside and out. The Normans quickly made use of the town's defensive capabilities and built a motte and bailey castle in the south-west corner of the defences, pulling down four houses in the process and taking over the site of the original church of All Saints. The new castle thus disrupted the simple layout of Warwick and has dominated the town's affairs ever since.

Warwickshire passed peacefully from Saxon to Norman rule, unlike many other parts of England. The main Saxon landowner in and around Warwick, Turchil of Arden – the 'Traitor' – failed to fight for King Harold at Hastings and King William let him hold on to his possessions. In about 1089 these lands were taken from Turchill's son and heir and given instead to the Norman *castellan* – or castle keeper – Henry de Beaumont or de Newburgh, who became the first Earl of Warwick. His son, Roger, took the surname de Warwick, supported the unfortunate King Stephen in the wars with Matilda, but surrendered Warwick in June 1153 to the future

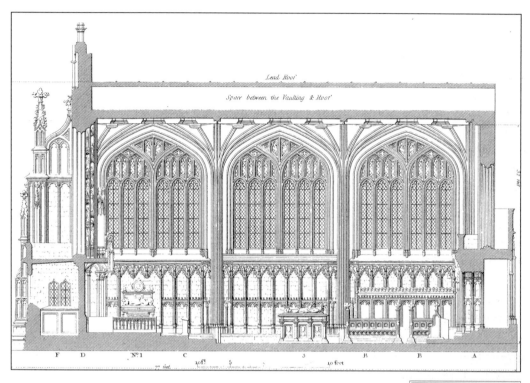

King Henry II. A later earl, William Mauduit, was loyal to Henry III in the Barons' Wars of the 1260s, but a small army of the rebel Simon de Montfort temporarily occupied both town and castle in 1264 – and took the ineffectual earl hostage. In 1268 the earldom and borough passed to Mauduit's nephew, William Beauchamp, and for the next two centuries the Beauchamp earls of Warwick dominated the affairs of the town and left the enduring legacy of much of the present castle, and the magnificent Beauchamp chapel in St Mary's church.

In the meantime, Warwick itself was continuing to develop. By the end of the thirteenth century the town was surrounded by a masonry wall and a ditch, probably on the line of the old Saxon defences. The first mention of a bridge occurs in 1208, which obviously improved the town's transport links, and a small suburban settlement grew up at the south end of the crossing, Bridge End. Other extramural settlements had grown

1 Detailed building surveys are not new. This fine cross-section through the Beauchamp Chapel and St Mary's by C. Wild was published in 1812. The quality of the details is excellent – putting the more mechanical computer-based surveys of today into perspective

up on either side of the main roads out of the town, and by
1279 the two market days, Wednesday and Saturday, are
mentioned. In the second half of the fourteenth century,
Warwick, like most of England, was hit by the successive
plagues known now as the Black Death, but appears to have
recovered relatively quickly.

When John Leland visited in the 1530s it was a reasonably
prosperous place, although the effects of Henry VIII's religious
transformations were beginning to be felt. The town's general
layout has changed surprisingly little since Leland's day. The
two long streets Leland mentioned met at the Cross, a medieval
stone structure, probably with an open ground floor. The
eastern part of the High Street is now called Jury Street. The
north–south road survives north of the crossroads as Church
Street and Northgate Street, blocked midway by the new tower
of St Mary's; to the south its line is followed by Castle Street,

3 Fine views of Warwick can be obtained either from the top of the tower of St Mary's or, as in this case, from the battlements and towers of the castle. In the foreground is the massive Guy's Tower, built late in the fourteenth century and, in the distance, St Mary's tower dominates the Warwickshire countryside. In between are the neo-classical castle stables, finished in 1771 after the castle grounds had been extended

but is then truncated by the extension of the castle grounds. The suburbs of Bridge End, Smith Street, Saltisford, and West Street were all well established. By this time the town probably had a population in the region of 2,500, which only increased slightly in the next hundred years or so.

In the Civil War, Warwick was, from the start, a key Parliamentary stronghold. The then earls of Warwick had no connection with the town at all. Instead Lord Brooke owned the castle and the allegiance of the town, and was one of the most important leaders of the Parliamentary cause. Shortly after the conflict began in 1642 an attempt was made to take the castle by Royalist troops under the Earl of Northampton. It was repulsed and Warwick was never threatened again. Instead, its castle became the main regional prison for Royalist troops. After the war, many castles up and down the country were 'slighted', often as punishment to Royalist sympathizers.

4 For centuries the commercial heart of Warwick has been its market place, seen here on a non-market day. Twice a week the stalls are still put out as they have been since time immemorial. In the background is the Market Hall and, to its left, the former Butcher's Market

5 A late nineteenth-century engraving of the West Gate, with Lord Leycester's Hospital on the right

6 Picturesque Mill Street once led down to the medieval bridge over the Avon. It not only escaped the Great Fire of 1694, but, due to the resiting of the bridge over the Avon a century later, it also escaped being modernized or devastated by twentieth-century traffic. The mix of brick, stone and timber-framing – by no means all of it genuine – coupled with the slight bend make this a very memorable streetscape

Lord Brooke's stately pile at Warwick survived. The Restoration of the monarchy had no adverse effect on the town, and within a few years a new Market Hall and Shire Hall had been built and its population had reached about 3,000.

Then catastrophe struck at the end of the long dry summer of 1694. September was always the most dangerous month in the timber-framed towns of England for fires. The Great Fire of London took place in September 1666, and Northampton was virtually destroyed in September 1675. Nearer at hand, Stratford-upon-Avon had been devastated by September fires in 1594 and 1595. In Warwick, on the afternoon of the 5 September 1694, a fire started at the west end of the High Street, near to the Friends Meeting House. A strong south-westerly breeze fanned the flames and the fire spread rapidly. One eyewitness account told how it was:

7 The ruins of the late fourteenth-century medieval bridge are clad with overgrowth and form a romantic eye-catcher from the castle. The bridge fell down soon after the New Bridge was opened further upstream in the 1790s

9

soe swiftly carried through the principal and chief tradeing parts of the Town, that within the space of half an hour, severall places, and farr distant from each other, were all in flames at once, soe that all endeavours that could be used to hinder the fierceness of its progress were vain and ineffectual

Within a few hours most of the High Street and Church Street, and parts of Jury Street, New Street and Castle Street, had been devoured by the blaze. Even the great church of St Mary's could not escape, and most of it was destroyed.

Almost immediately, a relief committee was set up under Lord Brooke and appeals were made to other towns to raise money to compensate those who had lost their homes and businesses. By the end of the year, an Act had been passed to regulate compensation claims and the manner in which the town was to be rebuilt. The opportunity was taken to improve

8 On the other side of the old medieval bridge was a once thriving suburb, called, not surprisingly, Bridge End. All the roads from the south met here but it became isolated at the end of the eighteenth century when the New Bridge was built. It is now an exceedingly pleasant and very quiet backwater

and widen the streets, and to create a new small square at the west end of St Mary's church. The new building lines were being staked out by the following summer and rebuilding quickly got underway. By the time Celia Fiennes passed through in 1697 she could already comment on the fact that the 'streetes are very handsome and the buildings regular and fine, [though] not very lofty being limited by act of parliament to such a pitch and size'. The town also tried to enforce high standards in the rebuilding to attract the rising gentry to live within the rebuilt centre of what was then the most up-to-date town in the Midlands. By 1716 Daniel Defoe could say that Warwick 'is now rebuilt in so noble and beautiful a manner, that few towns in England make so fine an appearance.'

Later in the eighteenth century, the separation of the castle and town was reinforced by the expansion of the castle

grounds. Prior to this, the main road south had passed the east wall of the castle as it led down the steep slope to the river to meet busy Mill Street at the approach to the bridge. On the other side of the river, three roads met at the southern approach to the bridge. Because of the constant repairs needed to the medieval bridge, Lord Brooke offered to pay for most of the cost of a new bridge – providing that it was built several hundred yards upstream, that the roads south of the river diverted to it, and that the old road running down the castle wall was closed. With all this agreed, the castle grounds were extended to the east between 1779 and 1785. Mill Street became a cul-de-sac, and the old suburb of Bridge End became isolated. Such are the trees around the castle grounds today, it is quite easy to forget, while in the town, that the castle exists.

Although Warwick did grow throughout the eighteenth century, it still did not expand or attract a great deal of industry

– even after the arrival of the canal in 1800. In the first half of the nineteenth century the town was overshadowed by the rapid growth of its near neighbour, the spa town of Leamington, which grew from a handful of houses and an hotel in 1800 to one of the most fashionable resorts in the country by 1850. While Leamington prospered, Warwick, despite its pleasant situation by the Avon, had a sufficiently high death rate to warrant being inspected under the auspices of the new 1848 Public Health Act. Piped water and new sewers were recommended for the county town.

By 1851 Warwick's population had grown, thanks in part to growth along the road to Leamington, to just under 11,000 people. Despite the arrival of the railway and more industry, it had only risen by another 1,000 people by the beginning of the twentieth century – during a period when most towns were experiencing very rapid growth, often doubling or tripling in

size. Even now, Warwick's population is only around the 23,000 mark, most of whom live outside the central area. This slow development has meant that the historic character of the place has survived remarkably intact.

Undoubtedly, Warwick's most important industry is now tourism, based mainly on the lure of its world-famous castle. The Brooke family that had owned the castle since the start of the seventeenth century were finally forgiven for their Parliamentary leanings in the Civil War when George III resurrected the earldom of Warwick in 1759 and conferred it on Francis Greville, Lord Brooke. By the nineteenth century the family, when not in residence, allowed people to look round their castle. The numbers wishing to do so rapidly increased, and now it is one of the most popular tourist attractions in the country, attracting in excess of 500,000 visitors a year.

Twice a week, Warwick's ancient Market Place comes alive as it has done for centuries – and it is good to see old-fashioned stalls selling up-to-date bargains out in the open instead of being cooped up in indoor shopping malls. Tourists still flock to Warwick, mainly to see the castle – though those who drive straight to its well-screened carparks and don't bother to look around the town that they can see from its battlements really do miss out on getting to know one of the most interesting towns in the Midlands. The one unwelcome effect of all these visitors is the traffic they create, and in Warwick, as in so many historic towns, this causes severe problems. Despite the newly finished bypass, traffic between the West and East gates seems to be an endless roaring stream that affects – literally – the atmosphere of the town. As long as the road transport lobby has the upper hand in national politics, and public transport is starved of the funds it needs and deserves, there will be no lasting solution to a problem that can only get worse.

After the Great Fire, the rebuilding of Warwick was well planned. The buildings on the corners of the central cross-roads were allowed to be of higher status than the rest. Three of these were houses, and the 'orders' of their pilasters were deliberately different. Working from the south-west corner clockwise, they were Doric, Ionic, and Corinthian. The Court House on the south-east corner, added later, was also Doric

Architectural Character

Warwick is a town of architectural set-pieces – the man-made medieval cliff of the castle rising sheer from the banks of the Avon; the nodding timber-framed gables of Lord Leycester's Hospital; the timeless tranquility of the 'lost' suburb of Bridge End; and the eighteenth-century elegance of Northgate Street, to name but a few. Even today, three hundred years later, the effect of the Great Fire of 1694 is still very much in evidence. After all, the heart of an essentially timber-framed town was ripped out and replaced by one of brick and stone in a new and uniform style of architecture based on symmetry and proportion.

The older, pre-Fire, Warwick can still be found on the periphery and in the former suburbs where timber-framing still dominates. Although the town is built, as Defoe described, 'on a solid rock of freestone, from whose bowels it may said to be built', until the Fire stone was a high-status building material. It was mainly used for major buildings such as the castle, the defences and the churches. Most other buildings were timber-framed, and timber here, on the edge of the far-famed Forest of Arden, was not in short supply.

Felled trees were measured and sawn in carpenters' yards and slotted together on the floor into the individual frames needed. The joints were usually numbered, commonly with Roman numerals cut or scratched into the face of the wood and usually now called carpenters' marks. Then the frames were dismantled, and the assorted pieces carted or dragged to the building site. Put back together, with the help of the

carpenters' marks, the frames could then be raised into position and the linking timbers, floors and roofs added. The panels in the resulting timber skeleton were filled in with wattle-and-daub, and, finally, plastered. They were not then painted black and white. The 'typical' magpie colour of timber-framed buildings is a largely Victorian tradition that is now beginning to be, thankfully, undone. Even so, more and more research into this type of building is producing, literally, a different and more colourful picture of how our medieval towns would have looked.

There are two main types of framing – the standard rectangular or square panelling and the more expensive close-studding. The medieval panels were often very large indeed, but gradually the size decreased until panels were quite small by the start of the seventeenth century and suited to ornate decoration. Close-studding – where upright timbers are placed

13 The fine array of timber-framed gables just inside the West Gate all now belong to Lord Leycester's Hospital. The original buildings are those beyond the stone archway; the nearer ones have been taken over in later years. The early seventeenth-century porch belonged to the former Anchor Inn, probably built a hundred years or so earlier. Nearer to the camera is a variation on the 'Wealden' type of late-medieval hall house, altered when the recessed hall was given a first floor and its front wall moved out in line with the jettied first floors of the wings

14 Park Cottage is on the very edge of the town, at the end of West Street. The jettied cross-wing with its close-studded first floor, probably dates to around 1500 but could be earlier. The side walls have typically large medieval panels, with braces to add rigidity to the framing

close together, often no more than a stud-width apart, was used in Warwickshire from the late-medieval period onwards. It was a deliberate show of wealth because of the cost of the timber involved and for this reason it was usually confined to the front frames of buildings. Where the side walls of such buildings are now visible, the difference between the public façade and the rest is quite striking.

Typical carpenters' marks still visible in the timbers of 10 Castle Street after several centuries

Excepting the Lord Leycester's Hospital, few of the timber-framed buildings in Warwick are particularly grand or flamboyant. Most of those in Bridge End, for example, are humble single-storey ranges with attics and few frills. This is not really surprising. The richer inhabitants mainly lived in the middle of the town and that is where the best buildings were. Such people would also be more likely to keep up with architectural fashions and rebuild. 'Warwick', said Defoe, 'was ever esteem'd a handsome, well-built town' before the Fire and

15 Close-studded timber-framing called for a great deal of timber and was usually only used for the public façades of buildings, the cheaper square-framing used for the side and back walls. In that respect, this sixteenth-century building, 49 West Street, is typical. What is not so typical is the very tall jettied first floor. The dormer gables on the front look suspiciously modern

would probably have had a wealth of ornately timber-framed buildings. Now only a handful of such buildings survive in the centre and perhaps the best example is actually on the outskirts, the Tudor House Hotel on West Street.

The average age of the surviving timber-framed buildings is also, in general, older than those found in other historic Midland towns. Again, this is because most are found in areas where the urge or the capacity to rebuild was not particularly great, the newer ones mainly perishing in the Fire. West Street is typical. In the early nineteenth century it was described as 'wide and airy, though principally consisting of low houses, inhabited by the working classes of the community', and that was probably always more or less the case. Now it can boast a fascinating collection of late-medieval and post-medieval timber-framed houses well worth much closer study.

The effect of the Great Fire on the architectural character of

16 At the bottom end of
Mill Street is this early
sixteenth-century close-
studded range, much
restored but conveying
the atmosphere of its
time well

Warwick was dramatic. The townspeople had to rebuild to strict rules laid down by an Act of Parliament passed in November 1694. This 'Act for the Rebuilding of the Town of Warwick and for Determining the Differences Touching Houses Burnt or Diminished, by Reason of the Dreadful Fire There' enabled Commissioners to be appointed to oversee the rebuilding work 'for the ornament, common convenience and safety of the borough'. The main streets were widened and owners compensated for the loss of their land, as well as for the damage done to their buildings. This gives much of Warwick its spacious appearance.

Houses were to be built of stone or brick and their roofs tiled or slated – timber and thatch were expressly forbidden. Most were only allowed to be of two storeys with attics, though some three-storeyed buildings, particularly near the centre, were allowed. Specific dimensions were imposed on the

heights of each floor – 10 foot high for ground and first floors, 8 foot high for the second floors. To try and prevent the spread of fire from house to house, party walls were to be at least 18 inches thick at ground floor level, 13 inches at the first and still 8 inches in the second floors and attics.

All these regulations were controlled by specially appointed surveyors – the forerunners of our modern planning officers – and by and large, were strictly enforced. One other important element in the rebuilding was the encouragement of local builders and architects and the fixing of the price of building work – all of which provided a vital boost to the town's devastated economy and also helped to enforce a pleasant harmony of style. Among the good craftsmen that benefited were carpenters such as William and Roger Hurlbutt, builders such as the Hiorns, and, above all, the architect/builder, Francis Smith.

17 Just saved from the flames, this corner building built in 1634 in the angle between New Street and Swan Street is one of the more ornamental of its period in the town. Multi-gabled, it has diagonal, or 'herring-bone', framing at first floor level and curved and diagonal braces in the attic dormers. The upper floors also have shallow jetties on both sides

18 The so-called Malthouse stands at the back of Lord Leycester's Hospital and probably dates from the sixteenth century. It has somewhat elaborate framing

19 Looking down Mill Street gives a good impression of how much of outer Warwick may once have looked in the seventeenth century, its streets lined with fairly irregular timber-framed buildings

Smith and his brother William were the sons of a Staffordshire bricklayer who had settled in Warwick. Due in no small part to the fire, they became successful builders. Francis, usually known now simply as 'Smith of Warwick', developed a successful architectural practice throughout the Midlands and, among other buildings, he designed part of Stoneleigh Abbey. Many of the post-Fire buildings in Warwick are probably by one or both of the Smith brothers but proof is generally lacking. The pair did rebuild St Mary's, and Francis built the new Court House and almost certainly designed 10 Market Place, Abbotsford House, for his father-in-law in 1714.

The Warwick that rose from the ashes is still pretty much the Warwick that survives today. It is, quite simply, the best example of a William and Mary town in Britain – for much of the rebuilding was done within ten years of the fire. The general design of the new houses, in either stone or brick,

was fairly standardized. Symmetrical façades, many five or more bays wide, were the rule, with slightly overhanging roofs with attic dormers in two-storey houses, low attic windows in the three-storey ones. Window openings were usually decorated by stone keystones and floors were marked by stone string-courses. The overall effect was of simplicity and refinement.

A handful of houses were allowed to be more ambitious, and at the site of the old Cross, those on three of the four corners were deliberately designed to act as a grand centre-piece to the town. Permission for these was granted in May 1695 and they were finished by the following year. Each is of three storeys, with attics, and each has pilasters supporting a decorated cornice of the same basic pattern. The pilasters of each house are of a different classical 'order' – the simple Doric on the corner of Castle Street and High Street, the voluted Ionic on

A late seventeenth-century doorcase with elaborate fanlight in Northgate Street

the corner of High Street and Church Street, and the florid Corinthian on the corner of Church Street and Jury Street.

   These three houses were built of brick, unfortunately now painted. The locally hand-made red brick is a pleasant, warm, material that harmonizes well with the local stone used for decoration. Only later did mass-produced machine-made brick from other areas and in varied colours become available – particularly after the arrival of the railway in the mid-nineteenth century. Brick had already been used to good effect before the fire, in Landor House just outside the East Gate for example, and may even have been used to clad some of the timber-framed buildings destroyed in the Fire. Hiding old-fashioned timber-framed buildings behind more up-to-date brick façades became common from the late seventeenth century onwards for owners unable to afford to rebuild completely. If even a brick façade was too expensive, timber-frames were often covered with lath-and-

21 Not everyone could afford the new architectural fashion for brick and symmetry in the eighteenth century and often only the front of a building would be rebuilt in the new material. This small late-medieval house in Gerrard Street is typical – its timber-framing still exposed behind a simple brick façade

plaster. Warwick has far fewer such examples than most historic towns – simply because of the Fire.

Not everyone built in brick after 1694, and the local stone was used in several of the better houses. It had been used for some of the larger houses, such as St John's and Marble Hill House, in the early seventeenth century but only became a relatively common material after the Fire. It was also, quite naturally, used for the more important public buildings. The stone is a Triassic sandstone, easy to work and cut when freshly quarried, and capable of taking decorative carving well. Unfortunately, it is also friable, and prone to weathering.

This defect can be seen in most of the stone buildings in Warwick. The Warwick Arms hotel is a typical example. Built in the last decade of the eighteenth century, its neo-classical design relies on proportion and austerity of decoration and the ashlar blocks of its façade should be tightly jointed. In the last

22 The Great Fire of 1694 stopped just short of this early seventeenth-century timber-framed house, now 12–14 Jury Street. Despite heavy restoration, and its unusual combination of a later neo-classical rusticated ground floor with jettied timber-frame above, it does show how many other buildings in the centre of Warwick might have looked before most of the town was reduced to ashes. Clearly the roundels in the framing were quite popular in Warwick

23 Even before the Fire, there was a hint of what was to come in Landor House, built just outside the East Gate in 1692. This shows the details of its cornice and overhanging eaves

two hundred years the edges (or, more technically speaking, the *arisses*) of the individual blocks have weathered and the joints are no longer crisp. The smooth architectural effect aspired to is impaired as a result. In several cases the stone has weathered to such an extent that whole façades have had to be replaced – which is why the Shire Hall, Gaol, Court House, and Abbotsford House all look to be in such pristine condition. They have each been refronted, in Hollington stone from Staffordshire, since the Second World War.

There is, inevitably, a conservationist dilemma here. Purists, following the Ruskin or William Morris line, would abhor such interference. Yet what else is there to do? Allowing a fine-fronted building to crumble away is surely not always the right answer. Patching with new stone seldom looks right, and it will take decades before the repairs begin to harmonize with the original work. Providing the original design is known, is

understood, is recorded, can be copied faithfully, and a well-matched stone, like Hollington, can be found, then surely in many cases this refronting is acceptable. The new front is, of course, a new front – but the overall effect will be what the original designer had in mind and the spirit of the building will have been saved.

Warwick's accidental lead in urban architecture and townscape was short lived. The town simply did not develop and expand and its architectural character remained predominantly domestic and unpretentious. There would be none of the grand terraces, squares or crescents so beloved by the later Georgians and, in nearby Leamington, the early Victorians. In fact, apart from a few more flamboyant nineteenth-century houses, particularly on the road to Leamington, Warwick's new developments have been very small in scale and ambition ever since.

25 Detail of a sash window of 22 Jury Street, another house built in stone after the Fire. The thin glazing bars of the sashes indicate that they were added much later

26 A 'Venetian' or 'Palladian' window of the mid-eighteenth century belonging to 27–9 Smith Street

27 Nos 18–20 Northgate Street are semi-detached houses built after the Great Fire. They share a pediment, but over the years different owners have had different ideas about how to repair the oval window within it

28 Warwick was rebuilt after the Great Fire at the same time that sash windows were beginning to usurp the earlier casements. This is a 'cross-mullioned' casement window belonging to 24 Castle Street – but a surprisingly late example for such a house as it was built in the middle of the eighteenth century

29 A late Georgian window in an ashlared and 'rusticated' façade. It belongs to the Judges' Lodging built alongside the Shire Hall in Northgate Street

30 This extremely grand window is in the Castle Street wall of Aylesford House, 1694. The date on the rainwater hopper shows how quickly the centre of Warwick was rebuilt after the Great Fire.

There have been some regrettable post-war changes, mainly around the Market Square. Until the 1950s the square was a proper country town square, a wide open space virtually surrounded by two and three-storey houses – the only larger building being the Market House to the south. At the end of the 1950s, the buildings at the north end of the square were demolished to make way for an extension to the Shire Hall and a gap was cut in the west side by Abbotsford House for an access road. To be fair, the Shire Hall extension (by G.R. Barnsley, opened in 1959) is not a bad building in itself. It would sit perfectly happily in its own landscaped grounds, approached by a driveway. But it does not sit well at the top end of Warwick's homely and historic market place. Once, for whatever reason, the decision had been made to demolish the houses at that end of the square, the planners were left with a dilemma. Today, when the frightened pseudo-vernacular school

31 Northgate House must be one of the most attractive purpose-built semi-detached houses in England. Designed to resemble a country mansion, it was started just after the Great Fire of 1694. The only real flaw in the composition is the central carriage-way. It is so nice to see such a building so well cared for – and just a pity that it now fronts on to a busy roundabout

26 The 'Venetian' window – a three-part design with an arched central window flanked by two narrower ones – was a typical motif of the English Palladian style. Usually such windows formed the centrepiece of a façade – but in 27–9 Smith Street, two flank a standard one in the middle. When this mid-eighteenth-century house was divided into two, a new door had to be added to the left of the original one – and the rusticated surround was copied exactly

of architecture reigns, it would not have been too surprising to see such an extension built behind a façade that looked like the houses that had been flattened to make way for it. That would clearly have been wrong. The character of the square was compromised once those houses had gone, and the building that replaced them should really, in retrospect, have been a lot more positive. Symmetrical, well proportioned, and in harmony with the rest of the square certainly, but a building that provided some sort of a focus to the open space, and a counterpoint to the Market Hall at the other end.

At that south end of the square, the wholesale redevelopment of Market Street in a bland, untidy and confused late-1960s manner is regrettable. More recent developments have been little different than those taking place in other similar towns throughout the country – neither particularly good nor particularly bad. Overall, Warwick has been lucky, and the

32 The Warwick Arms Hotel in High Street is a late eighteenth-century building faced with the local stone. Its neo-classical style calls for tightly fitted ashlar, but the nature of the stone has meant that the edges of the blocks, particularly in the upper storey, have been eroded and the effect is beginning to be lost

33 Abbotsford House, or 10 Market Place, is a magnificent example of the provincial version of the Baroque built in 1714 and almost certainly designed by Francis Smith. The front had to be completely refaced in 1963 because the original local stone had weathered so badly – as can be seen in the patched side elevation. It is doubtful that there were any alternative solutions to the problem

34 Later Georgian housing developments were not particularly successful in Warwick. These houses on the corner of Hampton Street and Crompton Street were built, probably in the 1820s, as part of an unsuccesful scheme to build a new suburb of middle class housing between the racecourse and West Street

35 Typical brick terraced and semi-detached artisan houses were begun in Warwick in the nineteenth century. Off Saltisford, Albert Street – together with the equally regally named Victoria and Edward streets – was laid out between 1901 and 1903

36 The 1960s extension at the back of the Shire Hall, facing the Market Place, is simply not a strong enough architectural statement for a building of its administrative importance. It needs something more. The way in which Abbotsford House has been incorporated into the offices is, however, sympathetic

37 In an age when multi-storey carparks are designed to resemble anything but multi-storey carparks, Warwick can boast a modern library complex that looks like a multi-storey carpark. This long concrete horror of 1983 ruins all the views of the town from Saltisford and is dangerously near the end of Northgate Street. No matter how well it works internally, in a town like Warwick the external design is simply not good enough

heavy hand of the unthinking urban developer has not lain too heavily upon it. Warwick has retained its historic character remarkably well, partly because for centuries it has not really been a particularly successful town and change has come only slowly. This, of course, gives it the very charm that now once again makes it attractive both as a tourist centre and as a very popular place to live. Planners are now very careful in what they allow to be done to the town's rich built heritage, and an active Warwick Society has a vitally important role to play in maintaining this unique town's charm.

Defences

The defences of Aetheflaeda's Saxon *burh* have proved elusive but are thought to have been followed by the town wall in the thirteenth century. The real strength of the town lay in its castle and the walls soon fell out of use, gradually being quarried for building stone. When Leland visited in the 1530s, he noted that the town 'hathe bene right strongly dykyd and waulyd, havynge the compas of a good mile within the wauls'; only fragments of the walls survived and the North Gate had gone. Today the situation is much the same, with short stretches of wall by the two remaining gates. A section in private gardens in The Butts includes part of a bastion.

The two gates are notable for the chapels built upon them. Indeed, approaching the West Gate, it is difficult at first to believe that it is anything else but a church, because the fifteenth-century tower of St James's rises from ground level and dominates the view. The present ribbed-vault gate-passage is cut into the living sandstone. The vaulting is of late fourteenth-century date, but clearly visible in the north wall are the semi-octagonal piers of an earlier vault of quadripartite form. In the south wall, the base of one answering pier survives, showing that the earlier passage, possibly contemporary with the building of the town wall, was of the same width. In the middle of the fifteenth century the chapel was given its west tower and the gate-passage had to be extended under it. When the chapel was being restored by Gilbert Scott in the 1860s, access round the east and south sides of the chapel was improved and the gate-passage was extended a little further eastwards.

At the opposite end of the town the East Gate has seen even greater changes since it was rebuilt in the fifteenth century. It

38 Warwick Castle's Caesar's Tower dominates this view of the castle, a view that would have greeted travellers crossing the medieval bridge. The gardens in the foreground are open as part of the National Garden Scheme and are well worth a visit in their own right, as well as for getting a different perspective on the castle

39 The Clock Tower is actually the castle's main gatehouse, built in the late fourteenth century by the Beauchamps and protected by a formidable Barbican in front of it. This main entrance to the castle could easily be made impregnable. To the left is Caesar's Tower, another splendid piece of military engineering, well ahead of its time

40 The best view of the inside of the castle is from the original motte, looking down on what was once its bailey. From left to right are Guy's tower, the Gatehouse, Caesar's Tower and, along the right-hand side, the main domestic quarters

was radically refaced and remodelled in the eighteenth century when Francis Hiorn was rebuilding St Peter's chapel. Little original work remains on view because of all the repairs and restorations, though the stone vaulting of the passage is of interest. The only reminder of the North Gate is in the name of the street, and of Northgate House.

Warwick Castle is described in its publicity leaflets as the finest medieval castle in England. It is neither an idle boast nor a new one. The diarist John Evelyn, writing in the seventeenth century, wrote that 'it may pass for one of the most surprising seats one should meet with.' In the middle of the last century a more flowery pen described what, to the early Victorians, was the perfect Romantic castle –

the embattled walls and grey sloping sides of the towers, descending with their mantling of ivy and lichens towards

the margin of the water offer a prolonged line of the best preserved and most striking castellated structure in England.

Much of the interior is Victorian too, because it suffered a devastating fire in December 1871.

The castle was lived in from the time it was first built right up until 1978. Many mourned the passing of the castle from family ownership into the hands of commerce, but it has to be said that Madame Tussauds have done an excellent job in making the castle a profitable and highly successful visitor attraction with an international reputation. Their fresh approach has brought the Victorian private apartments to life, capturing the spirit of a lost era in costume and wax. Purists may mock, but it works. What is more, it works without compromising the integrity of the rest of the castle, and the fact that it works helps pay for the upkeep of this priceless national asset.

41 The Bear and Clarence Towers may not look as dramatic as Caesar's or Guy's – but would have been if ever finished. They were part of a revolutionary artillery fortress begun by Richard III in the late fifteenth century, but work stopped after he was deposed

William the Conqueror's castle was a standard Norman 'motte-and-bailey', a new and effective military innovation virtually unknown to the Saxons. The motte was a tall mound, usually topped by a timber fighting tower which acted as a look-out and the last line of defence. The bailey was a defended enclosure next to the motte, surrounded by a ditch and rampart topped by a timber palisade. The palisade usually continued up the sides of the motte to meet another around the base of the fighting tower. The motte at Warwick still survives at the west end of the castle, and the general parameters of the present castle are probably the same as the original bailey. The timber defences and buildings were gradually rebuilt in stone during the twelfth century, and the old fighting tower on the motte replaced by a shell keep – a circular stone wall inside of which were a series of buildings against the masonry. This had ceased to be an important part

42 Several of the gaps between the 'merlons' – the standing up parts of the battlements – have been filled in at the western end of the castle and converted into gun-ports. This may have been carried out when the castle was made ready for action during the Civil War

of the defences by the time the castle was rebuilt in the fourteenth century, but was used as an artillery platform in the Civil War. The inner segment still survives, though much restored.

By the mid-thirteenth century the transformation from timber to stone was complete, but Warwick was still a fairly run-of-the-mill castle when it passed into the hands of the Beauchamps in 1268. They began a programme of expensive works that continued well into the fifteenth century and gave the castle much of its surviving medieval grandeur. Most of the work seems to have been carried out in the middle of the fourteenth century by Thomas de Beauchamp, the eleventh earl of Warwick and a close friend of Edward III – a king in love with chivalry. Thomas fought in the famous victories against the French at Crécy (1346) and Poitiers (1356). As well as being a Knight of the Garter and Marshall of England, he also

Somehow Madame Tussaud's have succeeded in the very difficult task of making an already popular tourist attraction even more so. The waxwork tableaux in the private apartments are really first class and bring the castle's late-Victorian prime to life. This is a scene in the Countess of Warwick's Gothick-decorated bedroom

became a very wealthy man because of the ransoms paid for his French prisoners – who included the Archbishop of Sens and the Bishop of Le Mans. This money helped in his rebuilding programme at Warwick, and its design shows that he had been influenced by what he had seen on his travels.

The main work concentrated on a magnificent show front at the east, flanking the main entrance and built as much with chivalric pomp in mind as mere defence. At either end are the two distinctive towers – Caesar's Tower to the south, and Guy's Tower to the north, both used as high class residences in peacetime. Caesar's Tower – once known as the Poitiers Tower because of the ransom money from that battle that helped pay for it – soars nearly 150 foot from the river bank to the top of its battlements. Its sheer size is impressive, but its design is even more so, being in many ways unique in England. Despite appearances, it is not a round tower, but lobate – then the height of military fashion and very difficult to build. At the top is another very rare feature, an embattled and slightly projecting balcony – or *'chemin de ronde'*, some distance below the top of the tower. Both balcony and tower top are machiolated – that is, they project slightly from the wall face below them, the overhang supported by stone corbels. Through the gaps between the corbels the defenders could drop burning pitch or quicklime, or just rocks, on top of anyone trying to scale the walls below. The machicolated were also found to be architecturally attractive and became used as much for baronial effect as for defence in the latter Middle Ages.

Guy's Tower, also machicolated, is a mere 128 foot high, and was certainly not finished on Thomas' death – though it probably had been started. It is named after a mythical Saxon Earl of Warwick – the same legendary figure commemorated in Guy's Cliffe, a few miles north of the town. In contrast to Caesar's Tower it is twelve-sided with five main storeys. Two completely separated spiral stone staircases – or vices – link the floors and the well-deserved reward for climbing these apparently interminable steps is one of the finest views in England. Guy's Tower was finished in the early 1390s by John Montfort, master mason to Thomas' son and heir, another Thomas.

In between the two towers the Gatehouse was also rebuilt. The five-storey Gatehouse is now also called the Clock Tower, for obvious reasons. Basically a tall square structure with residential rooms above the gate-passage, it has polygonal corner towers on the inside and rounded ones on the outside. In front is an additional, but lower, defensive structure over a vaulted continuation of the entrance passage, known as the Barbican, its entrance also flanked by polygonal towers. Only the most determined, or foolhardy, of attackers would even have contemplated a full frontal attack on this main entrance to the castle.

At the opposite end of the castle, the present Water Gate, or Ghost Tower, was also a part of the Beauchamp improvements. All the curtain walls were raised, and no doubt the domestic accommodation was improved and the Great Hall alongside the south wall rebuilt. The whole castle was considered to be one defensive unit guarded by its tall walls and taller towers. By

5 The formidable passage through the West Gate was partly cut through the sandstone rock on which Warwick is built. The ribbed vault was rebuilt in the late fourteenth century, replacing earlier quadripartite vaulting of which some of the semi-octagonal piers survive

44 Somehow the East Gate looks a lot less threatening than the West, even ignoring the Gothick chapel perched precariously on top of it. Nevertheless, it was still once a considerable deterrent to any attacker

the beginning of the fifteenth century, Warwick Castle must have been one of the grandest in all England, and was then owned by one of the most important men in England, Richard de Beauchamp, thirteenth earl, trusted friend of Henry V and the man for whose body the Beauchamp Chapel in the parish church was made. However, neither he nor his son, Henry, seem to have added to the basic fabric of the castle itself.

The next major change to the castle dates to the brief tenure of Richard, Duke of Gloucester, and left the Bear and Clarence towers on the north side. The castle had passed by marriage to Richard Neville, the notorious 'Kingmaker' whose actions during the Wars of the Roses eventually saw Edward IV confirmed as king – even though he had been held prisoner by Neville at Warwick at one stage. Neville married two of his daughters to the king's brothers, George, Duke of Clarence, and Richard, Duke of Gloucester. Clarence became Earl of

Warwick on Neville's death in 1471 but was executed in 1478 for plotting against the king. The castle and estates went to Gloucester, more famous – or infamous – as the usurper Richard III and the murderer of the two little 'Princes in the Tower'. Whether Richard was ever quite as bad as history – and Shakespeare – would have us believe is another matter. At Warwick he began a remarkable fortress within a fortress, clearly designed to defend not only against attack from those outside the castle – but also from those within.

The new building would have been as impressive as the great Beauchamp towers but was left unfinished at the end of Richard's brief, turbulent, reign. Unlike anything that had gone before, this square structure flanked by octagonal turrets was to be an artillery fortress, and several of the round gun-ports for the heavier guns remain. There was more strength than skill in the defensive arrangements, but if it had ever been finished it would have been a formidable obstacle to any attackers – and although much altered and reduced in size, it still stands as an important example of the most up-to-date military architecture of its time.

The accession of Henry VII ended the political chaos of the fifteenth century. Warwick remained a royal possession until Edward VI granted it to John Dudley in 1547, who was made Earl of Warwick at the same time on the grounds that he was the great-great-great-grandson of Richard, the thirteenth earl. Although he began rebuilding the domestic quarters on the south side, he too got caught up in national politics and, in particular, with the unfortunate Lady Jane Grey conspiracy. In August 1553 he lost his titles, his lands – and his head.

His son, Ambrose, was forgiven by Queen Elizabeth in 1561, and he probably continued the improvements at the castle. Elizabeth stayed here on the way to Kenilworth in 1572 with her retinue – a mere four hundred strong; there was no room left for the poor Earl and his family, who had to stay in a house in the town! After Ambrose died without heirs in 1590, the castle again came into the clutches of the Crown. James I gave it to Sir Fulke Greville in 1604, but not the earldom. That went, in 1616, to Robert Rich remaining in that family until the title died out in the eighteenth century even though they had no connection with town or castle.

45 Only a few sections of the town's medieval walls survive, such as this heavily rebuilt section just to the north of the West Gate

45 Over the years, new openings pierced the defences as the need for easy access overcame the need for defence. This little door was probably added in the sixteenth century, just to the north of the West Gate

When Fulke Greville, later the first Lord Brooke, took over the castle it was in a dilapidated state. He spent well over £20,000 on its restoration, adding new domestic ranges to the west of the existing ones and a new chapel. His son, Robert Greville, the second Lord Brooke, was a staunch Parliamentarian and Warwick Castle became a key stronghold for the Roundheads. Improvements were made to its defences – including the filling in of many of the battlements with gun-loops. Brooke was killed during the war but his castle was spared the destruction suffered by so many castles during and after the conflict. Ironically, his younger son, the fourth Lord Brooke, was one of the ringleaders in the Restoration of the monarchy in 1660.

For over three hundred years the Grevilles lived at the castle, and their association with the town was recognized in 1759 after the old line of the Earls of Warwick had died out. George III made the eighth Lord Brooke the first earl of a new creation, and the Earldom of Warwick was again synonymous with the castle. From the late seventeenth century onwards the Grevilles refurbished the interiors and altered them to the requirements of succeeding generations. In the late eighteenth century the external appearance of the castle was deliberately made to look even more medieval than it was, with miniature towers added to the remains of the masonry of the shell keep, a gateway created between the Clarence and Bear towers, and 'Gothick' windows added. More extensive alterations were needed after the fire of 1871 that severely damaged the Great Hall and gutted most of the private apartments. The rebuilding was carried out by Anthony Salvin, who had worked earlier at Windsor Castle.

Salvin's Great Hall, 62 feet long, is undoubtedly one of the highlights of the interior, but its detailing is a little mechanical and its stonework a little too crisp. Its impressive dark-timbered roof is actually made of painted pine. Other rooms may be a little humbler but are, architecturally, more interesting. The Cedar, Red and Green Drawing Rooms and the Blue Boudoir are particularly fine examples of late seventeenth-century interiors, started in 1669. The cedar panelling and carving is mainly by local men William and Roger Hurlbutt, the plaster ceilings by James Pettiver and a mysterious Mr Pelton, both of London. The State Dining Room was rebuilt in the 1760s by Thomas Lightoler, but much of its decoration – its early seventeenth-century-style ceiling and late seventeenth-century-style wainscoting, is peculiarly old-fashioned. Many of the remaining interiors date only to the late nineteenth century, but there are still many traces of centuries long-gone. What makes the interior of Warwick Castle memorable is its furnishing and fittings – the rich tapestries, grand fireplaces, splendid curtains, paintings and, of course, in the private apartments, the surprisingly life-like figures bringing to life a royal weekend party towards the end of the nineteenth century.

The castle stands in splendid grounds, sufficiently distancing itself from the town it once guarded. All this was helped by the closing of the old bridge and the street leading past the castle to it, and the extension of the castle grounds on all sides towards the end of the eighteenth century. Fulke Greville had started to create gardens around the castle in the early seventeenth century but these had been damaged by the defences needed in the Civil War. In the 1680s Evelyn had noted that the 'gardens are prettily disposed, but might be much improved'. In 1749 the necessary improvements were taken in hand by Lancelot 'Capability' Brown, in the new, naturalistic, fashion of garden design making use of what Evelyn had called 'a most goodly green, a woody and plentifully watered country . . . [with] . . . the river running so delightfully . . .' through it.

The gardens contain two buildings of note, the simple but handsome quadrangular late eighteenth-century stone stable block recently restored, and the Conservatory. This was originally called the Greenhouse and built in stone to a Gothick design with huge pointed windows by William Eborall in 1786. It was built to house the famous Warwick Vase, now stored rather more safely in Glasgow. As with most eighteenth-century conservatories and orangeries, it was not originally given a glazed roof; that was added in the nineteenth century, and the building itself was restored in the late 1980s.

Churches

Although there is no mention of a church in the Domesday Book, it is almost certain that there was at least one church, and probably several, in Warwick in the late Saxon period. The main church, All Saints, was in the south-west corner of the town on land taken over by the new Norman castle. In 1123 no less than nine churches are mentioned in Warwick – All Saints, St Helen's, St John's, St Lawrence's, St Mary's, St Michael's, St Nicholas's, St Peter's, and St Sepulchre's. Slightly later, there was also a St James's and a chapel at Mytton. This was a very large number of churches for a town of less than 2,000 people and it is not surprising that the numbers quickly fell.

The old mother church of All Saints was effectively united with St Mary's, which became the main church for the borough within the walls. St Nicholas', just outside the eastern defences of the town, became the other main parish church and the rest were allowed to fall into decay. Only when the town began to grow, in the early part of the nineteenth century, were new parishes created and new churches needed, a process accompanied by the growing numbers of non-conformist places of worship.

By far the largest, and oldest, of the town's churches is St Mary's. From a distance its tower, 174 foot high to the tips of its pinnacles, dominates the landscape and gives the town clustered around it the appearance of a small cathedral city. The tower was the last major part of the fabric to be built, perhaps 800 years after the church was started. There are no traces of any Saxon work in the present structure, and only the impressive crypt beneath the chancel remains of a great Norman church started in the early twelfth century. In 1123 the new church became collegiate, that is, it supported a team, or

1 The tall tower of St Mary's dominates the upper Avon valley, but despite its medieval appearance it was built several years after the Great Fire of 1694 destroyed most of the earlier church. The first design for the tower failed, and it had to be hurriedly re-sited to the west of the planned west end of the church

1 Robert Skyllington was probably responsible for designing the nave of St Mary's in the late fourteenth century, and it miraculously survived the Great Fire. Of particular note are the flying ribs of the vaulting, certainly individual if not exactly aesthetically pleasing

1 One of the most famous medieval set-pieces in England, the fourteenth-century Beauchamp Chapel was also one of the most expensive works of architecture for its size of its day. It was built to house the mortal remains of Richard Beauchamp, Earl of Warwick, who died in 1439, and some of the finest craftsmen of the time worked on it

college, of canons under the leadership of a dean. Later it acquired its own Vicars Choral and a Choir School.

The church benefited from the Beauchamp dynasty and in the late fourteenth century the chancel was rebuilt, along with the chapter house. The work may have been carried out by the master mason Robert Skillyngton between 1381 and 1396 and the chancel, in particular, is a fine tribute to medieval craftsmanship and innovation. Tall and graceful, it is a fairly early example of the last native development of the true Gothic style – aptly known now as the Perpendicular. The vaulting is somewhat unique, with spectacular flying ribs creating an odd three-dimensional effect. The original feel of the adjacent chapter house, a place to meet and discuss the day-to-day running of the medieval college, has been lost because it was chosen as the site of the first Lord Brooke's tomb in 1628. The tomb itself is simple and elegant – but clutters up the space.

The most famous part of the church is undoubtedly the Beauchamp Chapel, 'right fayre, large and somptuus' and one of the best examples of Perpendicular architecture in the country. It was built as the chantry chapel of Richard Beauchamp, who died in 1439, so that priests could pray for his departed soul. This attempt to buy his way into heaven cost the earl's heirs the staggering sum of £2,481 4s 7½d and the chapel, begun in 1443, took over twenty years to complete. The accounts are remarkably intact. The masonry work was probably supervised by Thomas Kerver of Warwick, the woodwork was contracted to two Londoners, Richard Bird and John Haynes, and the stained glass windows to John Prudde, the royal glazier. Perpendicular Gothic works better on the grand scale, often best seen from afar. In this relatively small chapel its effect is a little predictable and a little overpowering – but this is more than compensated for by the tomb itself and the astonishingly life-like gilded brass effigy of the earl. The long, delicate, veined hands are particularly noteworthy and the model used for the casting was either by John Massingham or John Essex; the casting itself was made by William Austen of London.

The Beauchamp Chapel was built on the site of the Deanery, and in between it and the chancel is a tiny architectural gem, the Dean's Chapel. Its miniature fan vaulting is almost a toy-

1 Between the Beauchamp Chapel and the Chancel is the absolutely delightful Dean's chapel, with its toy-like vaulting. It was probably fitted out in this manner in the mid-to-late fourteenth century, but much of its intricate decoration and its statuary was defiled by Parliamentary soldiers in the Civil War

1 Inside the rebuilt section of St Mary's, the nave and its aisles are all of the same height, and the slender columns dividing them help to retain an atmosphere of space and light. The style is essentially late-Gothic, but also uses neo-classical motifs. Only the ugly windows detract from the quality of the overall design

like version of the splendour of Henry VII's chapel at Windsor – but was built many years before.

Apart from losing its collegiate status during the religious upheavals of the early sixteenth century, the church was otherwise unharmed until the Civil War, when puritan fanatics destroyed much of the remaining statuary and stained glass. Then, in the Great Fire of 1694, the nave, aisles, transepts, and tower of the medieval church were either destroyed or damaged beyond repair. Tradition has it that some salvaged furniture brought to the church for safety was still smouldering, caught light, and set fire to the church. A more likely cause would have been sparks from the inferno setting fire to the timbers of the roof.

Funds were quickly raised to allow it to be rebuilt and Roger Hurlbutt put a temporary wooden roof over the chancel to protect it. The town itself put up £11,000 and Queen Anne

46 The Gothick west door of St Nicholas' was built in 1748 and would have been the height of fashion, on a par with Walpole's 'Strawberry Hill Gothick'

donated £1,000. The famous architect, Sir Christopher Wren, drew up at least one design for the rebuilding, but Sir William Wilson was given the task of reconstruction instead. He was no aristocrat by birth, but a simple sculptor from Leicester who had married well. It could be argued that he was no architect either. St Mary's is his only noted work, and in 1700 his new tower, then only 30 foot above the roof of the new nave, was beginning to crack. This was because he had used the local Warwick sandstone, and it simply couldn't stand the weight. The tower was taken down and the present one built, with Shrewley stone, to the west of the nave. Its lower portion has arched opening in three sides so as not to hinder the pedestrian traffic in the planned new square. The contractors for the work were William and Francis Smith, and the church was ready by 1704.

Inside, the new plaster-vaulted nave and aisles are, unusually, of the same height and separated by quite slender four-shafted columns. This creates a tremendous feeling of space. The style is an odd combination of the Perpendicular Gothic and stray classical motifs, typified by the acanthus leaf capitals of the otherwise quite medieval columns. It is difficult to categorize. It is not really Gothic Revival, or even Gothic Survival; perhaps it is how English Gothic may have developed if it had been left to its own devices. Attitudes to Wilson's work have changed over the years. Defoe, writing shortly after it was re-opened, considered that 'The new church . . . is a fine building', but a hundred years later one writer called its architecture a 'singular, and indeed, absurd mixture of different modes'. That judgement now seems somewhat unfair, but his comment that the undoubtedly ugly windows are the result of 'the strange violation of all architectural rules' cannot be denied; they are truly awful.

In 1976 St Mary's was united with the other long-serving medieval parish church, St Nicholas's, and both are now served by a team ministry. St Nicholas's used to be called the 'low' church – not because of the type of services it offered, but simply because it was physically lower than St Mary's, the 'high' church further up the hill. The old church dated back to Norman times and may have been earlier still, but by the mid-eighteenth century it was in a poor state of repair. The tower, in

5 The Guild Chapel over the West Gate was heavily restored by Sir George Gilbert Scott in the 1860s, at which time it was in danger of collapse. Scott had to be quite brutal in his work. It was also Scott who added the balcony on the south side of the church to give better access to the main entrance

5 The inside of the Guild Chapel is still lit by candle-light and still used daily by the members of Lord Leycester's Hospital. Most of the visible work is of the 1860s

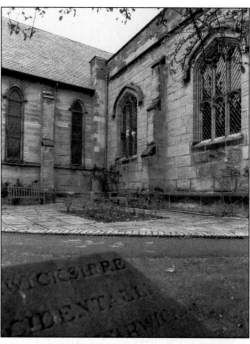

44 The small chapel of St Peter's perched on top of the town's East Gate was a medieval foundation but the present building was opened in 1788. Designed by Francis Hiorn it is a pretty and playful eyecatcher from either approach to the gate, with classical symmetry and Gothic details

47 St Paul's church on Friar's Street started life as a mortuary chapel for a graveyard in 1825. Later it became a church in its own right and was radically extended at a cost of £3,500 and with stone provided by the Earl of Warwick. The old chapel became an unusually long south transept, seen here on the right hand side

particular, was causing concern and was taken down and replaced by another, with a spire, in 1748. Thirty years later it was decided to take the rest of the church down and rebuild that too to a design by local architect Thomas Johnson. Work began in 1779 and the church was re-opened on 17 September 1780. There has been some debate as to whether the new tower was refaced at the same time. The visible evidence suggests that it was not, even though the new masonry was carefully chosen to match. The outline of the tower's buttresses can clearly be seen where the tower and the main body of the church meet. In addition, the decoration of the tower is copied from Decorated Gothic, while the rest is an attempt at aping the Perpendicular.

The rebuilt church is an early example of a relatively serious attempt at the Gothic Revival, making the even earlier tower something of an unsung architectural landmark. Writers in the

48 All Saints church in Emscote takes its name from the original Saxon mother church of Warwick, built on the site of the later castle. The dramatic modern church replaced a rather fine Victorian church by James Murray opened in 1856 and enlarged in 1872. In the background is the school built in 1887, in honour of Queen Victoria's Jubilee

early nineteenth century, when medieval ecclesiastic Gothic was being taken very seriously indeed, were quite scathing about Johnson's work. One vilified it as 'a lamentable specimen of modern gothic . . . a wretched jumble of different styles, and in no part . . . a single instance of correct taste or judgement'. Another, more diplomatically, said simply that it was 'not admired as being in good taste'. There is, certainly, enough to annoy the Gothic purist – the slightly odd use of motifs and the plaster vaults inside for example, and the pyramidal roof over the nave – but all in all the church is rather attractive and has a very pleasant, almost park-like, graveyard. A vestry was added in 1826 and the chancel was rebuilt in 1869–70, to the designs of John Gibson.

Warwick is probably unique in still having two gate chapels. The first mention of St James' chapel is in 1123. It was given by Thomas Beauchamp, Earl of Warwick, to the

51 The Quakers are noted for their humble places of worship, and the Warwick Meeting House off High Street is no exception. The Great Fire started around this point, destroying their old quarters. The present brick building was built soon afterwards and has retained many original features – such as the cross-mullioned casement windows

50 Compared to all too many historic towns, Warwick has had a generally good record in looking after its historic buildings – but the condition of the Master's House in Saltisford is a disgrace. Built for the master of St Michael's Hospital in the fifteenth century, it later became converted into smaller houses. Clearly it has been 'restored' at some time in the recent past, but it has been derelict now for several decades

new Guild of St George formed in 1383 and became their chapel, and later the chapel of the United Guilds of Warwick. It seems likely that the chapel was rebuilt at this time over the rebuilt gatepassage, though only the walls of that chapel survive. The west tower that forms such a dominant feature of the western approach to Warwick was added in about 1450. The chapel was ruinous by the late sixteenth century, by which time it was a part of Lord Leycester's Hospital, and the east window was blocked. Despite being repaired it was again in a poor state by the mid-nineteenth century and was radically restored between 1863–5 by Sir George Gilbert Scott, one of the most famous and most respected architects of his day.

Scott rebuilt the upper parts of the walls, completely rebuilt the low-pitched roof, designed a new east window in what had, for centuries, been a blank wall, and added rather plain Tudor Gothic windows in the side walls. At the same time, he added a buttressed walkway on the south side of the chapel to allow easy access into the south door. Most of the carved woodwork inside the chapel dates from this restoration, and it also contains some William Morris tapestry of the same period. The glass in Gilbert Scott's east window is by Clayton & Bell of London. The overall result is very pleasant, and one rather nice feature of the restored chapel is the fact that it is lit only by candle-light. It is used every day by members of the Hospital.

Scott's restoration of St James' chapel was a serious one, following strict Gothic guidelines as far as was practicable. At the opposite side of town, the chapel over the East Gate is of a completely different character. The earlier chapel of St Peter's over the gateway probably dated to the mid-fifteenth century but was ruinous by 1571. It survived, though much altered and in a deteriorating state, until the late eighteenth century when a decision was made to rebuild it. The architect was a local man, Francis Hiorn, three-times mayor of Warwick and noted for his experiments with the Gothic style. The result, finished in 1788, is decidedly playful when compared to Scott's, more Gothick than Gothic but a fine eye-catcher at the end of the long vista of Jury Street. The chapel is now part of the Girls' High School.

49 The little chapel of the medieval St Michael's Hospital in Saltisford is in the process of being restored – and the repairs have had to be quite comprehensive. In fact, it looks as though most of the external masonry is being replaced

Warwick, like most medieval towns of its stature, had other religious buildings besides parish churches and chapels. By the twelfth century it had a priory, St Sepulchre's, and three Hospitals, St Lawrence's (for lepers), St John's, and St Michael's. A Dominican friary was started in the 1260s, and in Bridge End there was St Helen's chapel and hermitage. Virtually nothing survives of any of these establishments above ground, mainly because of the Dissolution. Remarkably, two buildings connected with St Michael's Hospital, Saltisford, still stand – though only just. The small stone chapel with its trussed rafter roof and Tudor windows was described by Leland as being 'much in ruin' in the 1540s and was later incorporated into an eighteenth-century cottage. It is now being rather radically restored. Close by is the shamefully neglected building known as the Master's House. This close-studded two-

52 The Unitarian Chapel in the High Street is not an architectural masterpiece. Indeed, it is decidedly plain. The chapel was resited here when the castle grounds were extended, and is mainly of 1781 vintage – but the ugly windows are Victorian

storeyed timber-framed building probably dates to the fifteenth century and was extended in the seventeenth century. At one stage it was divided into three cottages, but there is some evidence that an attempt was made in the nineteenth century to restore it. Sadly, it has clearly been derelict now for several decades and it is surprising that it is still up. It is quite shocking that a building of this type, a rare example of a medieval domestic building attached to a hospital, should have been allowed to get into this condition. It simply has to be saved.

In 1825 a mortuary chapel opened in the cemetery off Friars Street. It was a simple but substantial affair built in a late

53 The former Congregational Chapel in Brook Street is no longer used for worship and has been converted to offices. The plain stuccoed front was part of Thomas Whitewell's extension to the mid-eighteenth-century chapel in 1826

Perpendicular style with quite large windows. In 1849 it became a suburban parish church, dedicated to St Paul. A new nave and apse were added across the north end of the old chapel, effectively making that the south transept of the enlarged church. The new work is in a much meaner, vaguely Early English, style with tall lancet windows and little decoration.

In 1861 a new chapelry of All Saints was founded in Emscote, based on a church of that name built between 1854–6 by James Murray. This was radically enlarged in 1872 and in the next few years a vicarage, curate's house, hostel (St

54 The Roman Catholic church of St Mary Immaculate on West Street was designed by Edward Pugin and opened in 1860. The spirelet-topped bellcot is a typical feature of his work, the quality of which was rather uneven. In this case the heavy round west window spoils the effect

Edith's) and school were all added. This rather fine Victorian church was found to be in need of considerable repair in the post-war years and was taken down. Only the school and St Edith's hostel still stand by the new and unashamedly modern church.

Non-conformity has a long history in Warwick, but none of their surviving buildings call for much comment. The best is also the humblest and oldest, and belongs to the Quakers. The Society of Friends owned a plot of land off the High Street for burials in the 1670s and had a meeting house on the site – probably a converted timber-framed house or barn. The Great

Fire of 1694 started nearby and it was destroyed. Almost straight away, plans were made to rebuild, and a new meeting house was finished in 1695 at a cost of under £117. Built of brick, with stone quoins, stone plinth, and a plain-tiled roof, this typically humble building still stands, tucked away in its own secluded courtyard away from the busy street. It has been altered on occasion, and in the late eighteenth century a cottage was added to the west end. Inside, the fittings include a gallery and some eighteenth-century panelling and it is nice to see the original cross-mullioned windows with their small rectangular 'quarries' of glass still surviving. The building virtually ceased to be used for meetings in 1912, but was reopened in 1949 by Friends from Leamington and since 1954 meetings have become regular once more.

The mid-nineteenth century saw the emergence of Roman Catholicism on a big scale following centuries of persecution. In Warwick, the Catholic church of St Mary Immaculate was built in West Street in 1860. It was designed by Edward Welby Pugin, a man with a famous name (the son of the famous Augustus Welby Pugin) but not a famous talent. The red-brick neo-Gothic church with its steep slated roof is decorated with Bath stone and boasts a large rose window to the street and a small bellcot with echoes of rural France.

Public Buildings

Warwick has been an administrative centre for well over a thousand years, ever since the creation of the Saxon county of Warwickshire in the early tenth century. The borough's own affairs were largely controlled by the Earl himself throughout most of the medieval period, and the first charter was not granted until 1545. This granted more power to the townspeople, and also transferred to them many of the functions that had gradually been taken on by the semi-religious Guilds.

The Guild of St George was formed under licence from Richard II in 1383, thanks to the patronage of Thomas Beauchamp who also granted them the chapel of St James. At an unknown date, but before 1413, the Guild of the Holy Trinity and the Blessed Virgin had moved from St Mary's church and combined with the Guild of St George, the two bodies being known simply as the United Guilds. These types of medieval guilds were effectively self-help groups, looking after not only the spiritual, but often the physical, needs of their members – and of the township as a whole. In order to cater for their growing role, a series of timber-framed buildings were built just to the north of the West Gate and the rebuilt chapel and, thankfully, these survived both the Dissolution and the Great Fire. Religious guilds fell victim to Henry VIII and his Commissioners, but the swift thinking of the then Master of the Guild, Thomas Oken, in transferring the Guild's property to the town saved the buildings. For a while they were used for borough business

13 The splendid courtyard of Lord Leycester's Hospital is not quite all that it seems. Three of the four sides are indeed medieval, but the fourth, and grandest, is not. The Master's House, in the background, was in a poor state in the mid-nineteenth century and a new front was added to it – of brick with raised plaster 'framing'

but in 1571 the Earl of Leicester, Queen Elizabeth's favourite Robert Dudley, acquired the site. He founded the Hospital for twelve retired or infirm soldiers or seamen that still bears his name – though always spelt in the old-fashioned way – and Lord Leycester's Hospital was still run under the terms of its original charter until 1956. The buildings were then found to be in a shocking state and between 1958 and 1966 much of the framing was taken down, repaired or replaced, and then put back up again. The old charter was repealed by Act of Parliament and the eight ex-servicemen and their wives are now housed in a rather more up-to-date fashion.

13 The grand timber-framed medieval Great Hall of Lord Leycester's Hospital has been hosting public events since the end of the fourteenth century when it was built by the Guild of St George. It was originally heated by an open fire burning on a central hearth, the smoke eventually finding its way out through a louvre in the roof

The architectural legacy of the United Guilds is a fine one, and few towns can boast such a quadrangle of medieval timber buildings. The oldest is on the west side of the courtyard, the fine Great Hall probably built soon after the formation of the

5 The United Guilds' private Guildhall is on the first floor of the south range and was the place where the day-to-day running of their affairs was discussed. The table is said to be original. When the hospital was founded, this hall was divided into four apartments and remained that way until 1950

55 If it were not for the oppressive and over-heavy glazing inserted into its once open ground floor arcading in about 1880, Warwick's Market House would be a very handsome building indeed. Designed by William Hurlbutt in 1670 it was taken over by the County Council in 1937 and is now an attractive and, to the credit of all concerned, free museum

Guild of St George. Originally it was entirely timber-framed, the lower stone portions clearly being a later repair on the courtyard side. The west wall, incidentally, is a good example of a complete, modern rebuild. The plain but large roof, with its braced trusses, gives a real feel of how a medieval hall would have looked – if you could have seen much of it through the smoke billowing up from the central hearth towards the louvre in the ridge. The Great Hall has been used for public functions for 600 years – and still is.

Another hall, this time a first floor one, occupies much of the south side. This, the Guild Hall, was, as its name suggests, used exclusively by members of the guilds and was probably built about half a century later than the Great Hall. It can boast a fine arch-braced roof and close-studded timber-framed walls. Amazingly, when the Hospital took over, this was divided quite roughly into four dwellings – and remained so until 1950. A

56 The ground floor arcade of the former Shambles or meat market has also been filled in and the eighteenth-century building in the Market Place is now the Tilted Wig

doorway from the hall leads into the east range, though the two were built as completely separate buildings.

In many ways the east range is, architecturally, the most interesting. It consisted originally of two large rooms, one on either floor, served by open passages at each level on the courtyard side. The southern part of the ground floor now serves as the Brethren's Kitchen, a more than interesting enough place for a meal or a pot of tea. The upper floor, another first floor hall known as the Priest's Dining Room, is open to one of the most unusual roofs in the region. One early form of high status medieval roof was the crown post. There were no trusses, as, for example, there are in the Great Hall. Instead, the tie-beams carried a central post which, in turn, supported a longitudinal beam or purlin. All of the rafters were paired and joined by a horizontal piece known as a collar. Such rafters are called, confusingly, trussed. The

57 The Court House was designed by Francis Smith in the 1720s. It is certainly a striking Palladian building but the banded rustication should really have been confined to the ground floor. Using it all over the façade makes the building a little too fussy and detracts from a well-proportioned design

58 The west side of Northgate Street has, side-by-side, two of the finest public buildings in the Midlands. In the background is the Shire Hall, opened in 1758, and designed by Sanderson Miller. Nearer to the camera is the more austere façade of the gaol, opened in 1783 – Thomas Johnson's uncompromising design deliberately impressing on would-be criminals the sheer weight of the law and its retribution

59 The pedimented portico of Miller's Shire Hall. The building has had to be refaced because of stone erosion, but the original design was adhered to in the new work

Around the corner from the main entrance to the former gaol is this little door in Barrack Street, a grim reminder of what the building was for

collars then sat on the central purlin. This type, in the Midlands at least, gradually gave way at the end of the fourteenth century to the truss type of roof in which proper trusses support pairs of side purlins, that, in turn, support the rafters – and these no longer have to be trussed themselves. The roof of the Priest's Dining Hall is somewhere between the two styles. At either end there are normal crown posts, but these are part of fully developed trusses carrying side purlins. The intermediate trusses are quite high, and the crown posts they carry are almost toy-like. Even stranger, the side purlins have to be supported on tiny bits of timber resting on the truss. It really is most peculiar.

The most striking building in the courtyard is the Master's House on the west side, the only part that is still 'black-and-white'. There is a real medieval building there, but this front wall was only put up in the mid-nineteenth century and the 'timbers' are in fact raised and painted plaster on a brick carcass. The busy design was copied from the nearby Malthouse, a secular building taken over by the Hospital in antiquity. Another building, on the High Street, also now belongs to the hospital, the former Anchor Inn, dating to the early sixteenth century.

For many years the affairs of Warwick's ancient market were organized from a Booth Hall, but by the mid-seventeenth century this was getting rather dilapidated and a subscription fund was opened to raise money to build a new one. The Market Hall was designed by William Hurlbutt, and opened in 1670. It is one of the best examples of its time, but although it is now well-adapted to serve as the county museum, it has had a less-than-secure past. Built of the local sandstone, it has the typically large and overhanging roof of the period. Originally, like most such buildings, its arcaded ground floor was open and market stalls could shelter within. There was also a small lock-up, used until 1848, and, on the first floor, a large meeting room.

In 1836 the newly formed Warwickshire Natural History and Archaeological Society took over the first floor and later the entire building, creating a museum and infilling the ground floor in the process. A century later the building was in drastic need of repair and was offered to the County Council in 1932. Shortly afterwards, there were – amazingly – plans to demolish it. Sympathies change, and the building was restored in the 1960s, when its dormers and lantern were put back. The only things that let this fine structure down aesthetically are the Victorian windows infilling the arcade. Usually, and quite rightly, every piece of a building's history should be retained, as far as possible – buildings are, after all, organic things that develop over the centuries. In this case should those appalling windows really stay? Can't they at least be replaced by something a little more sympathetic to this rare example of Restoration architecture?

The present Court House, aptly enough on Jury Street, was the last of the four grand buildings put up at the ancient Cross after the Great Fire. While the three houses on the other corners were ready within a few years, the corporation only started on the Court House in the mid-1720s and it was

finished in 1731 at a cost of £2,253. Although designed primarily for corporation business, one group of locals claimed it was used only for wining, dining and gambling, and complained that it had been financed by money meant for local charities. A suit of Chancery was filed and the corporation ordered to pay back the money; they couldn't, and the building was sequestrated in 1742, leaving the corporation to meet in a local hostelry for the best part of thirty years!

The architect was Francis Smith, once again using local stone. The design is essentially Palladian but rather odd. The deliberate incising of deep 'joints' into ashlared stonework is known as 'rustication', and was usually confined to the lower floors – sometimes known as the rustics – to make the upper floors look taller and grander as if they were the temples sitting on top of their plinths. Here, Smith rusticated the first floor as

62 The poorly poor generally had to rely on charity to cure their illnesses. In 1826 this early eighteenth-century house in Castle Street was taken over and converted into a Dispensary financed by voluntary subscriptions

63 Although coffee houses enjoyed a rather rowdy reputation in eighteenth-century England, when they reappeared briefly in the late nineteenth century they were closely associated with the Temperance Movement. Warwick's Coffee Tavern in Old Square was built in 1880

well, between the Doric pilasters, and this not only tends to make the stonework a little too busy, but the emphasis on horizontal banding detracts from its fine proportions. Inside, the first floor is mostly given over to the elegant Ball Room that was, for many years – after being restored to the corporation – an important part of town life. The external stonework was largely renewed in 1960, and the original design of parapet, replaced in the nineteenth century, has been restored.

Warwick is fortunate to have two excellent examples, side by side, of the type of public buildings needed for its other administrative role – that of a county town. The 1694 fire did not damage the west side of Northgate Street, where the old Shire Hall, rebuilt by William Hurlbutt in 1678, stood. Nevertheless, by the mid-eighteenth century it was decided to replace it and the amateur architect, Sanderson Miller, designed the new building. The new Shire Hall took five years to build and opened in 1758. Built of local stone by local men David and William Hiorn, it is an elegant neo-classical building of nine bays with an attached three-bay – or tertrasyle – Corinthian portico. Inside it is equally fine, with one huge full-height chamber along the front with two pillared octagonal courtrooms projecting to the rear. During Warwick Races, a dance floor was laid over the flagstones in the main room and the courtrooms were converted to card rooms. The stone facing of the façade had to be renewed entirely in Hollington stone, the work being completed in 1948.

Next door to the Shire Hall is the façade, and it is only the façade, of the former gaol. This was built between 1777 and 1783 to the designs of Thomas Johnson of Warwick, and in the same local stone; it was refaced shortly after the Shire Hall. The design is suitably sombre, almost brooding, with plain Doric, rather than Corinthian, portico and pilasters. In fact, it is even more severe than it was originally meant to be – the architect's model showed the columns were to be fluted, but for some reason they were left plain. In reply to complaints that he had not fulfilled his contract, Johnson claimed that the Justices wanted plain columns, and plain they have stayed. It is considered to be one of the earliest

examples of the use of the Greek Doric order on an English public building – something that became very popular by the end of the century. The gaol was extended to a new and plain Barrack Street façade between 1790–3 by Henry Couchman. That street gets its name from a later use of the gaol – the prisoners were replaced by the soldiers of the First Warwickshire Militia in 1861. At that time the three arched openings were made in the central portico. The County Council took over the site later and between 1929 and 1932 built an office complex behind the two main façades – so much so that virtually nothing is left of the original work. Oddly enough, within the complex is a brutal remnant of the earlier seventeenth-century gaol – an octagonal dungeon built in 1680 and only abandoned in 1797.

Warwick has a variety of other public buildings, though few are of exceptional architectural quality – and some, like

the Post Office of 1886 on Old Square, are decidedly unattractive. The town has a long history of education but this is hardly reflected in the surviving buildings. Warwick School moved to its present site on the Myton Road in 1879 into a vaguely Jacobethan pile designed by J. Cundall. The Girls' High School opened in the same year in Landor House by the East Gate and now occupies a variety of buildings, some purpose built, others, like St Peter's chapel, decidedly not.

65 Warwick School moved to the Myton Road site over the Avon in 1879 into a neo-Jacobean building designed by J. Cundall. It has continued to expand ever since

Houses

Warwick can boast a rather good and varied collection of houses built from the medieval period onwards – although these have had to adapt over the centuries to change. The spaciousness of the town's streets is reflected in many of its houses. In most medieval towns, the demand for housing in the centres was enormous with everyone wanting to be on the main streets. This led to the creation of the typical narrow burgage plots running back at right angles to the streets – often subdivided into even narrower strips as the pressure on building land increased. This, in turn, resulted in the typical streetscapes of tall, narrow, buildings – often still apparent today after most of the buildings have been rebuilt several times. In much of the centre of Warwick, this does not seem to have been the case. Instead, the buildings all seem to have had more room and wider street frontages. This could reflect the town's relative lack of commercial success but also has an important effect on the architecture of the houses and the general feel of the town.

The link between town and country was always very close in towns such as Warwick, and the medieval town house was usually very similar to those built in the country, simply adapted to fit the more restricted urban property boundaries. The surviving medieval houses in Warwick are, for obvious reasons, on the periphery or straggling along the sides of the old main roads outside the old town walls.

The medieval house, as opposed to the short-lived medieval hovel that was home to the majority of the population, revolved around the one communal room – the hall. The typical hall was a tall, single-storey room open to the roof, heated by an open fire in the middle of the floor whose smoke had to find its way up through a louvre in the roof. The hall

66 At the end of Jury Street, close to the East Gate, is this unconvincing, but quite jolly, mock-timber-framed front of No. 37 – dated 1856 on the hopper head. Behind the façade, however, is the remnant of a medieval house that may date to the fourteenth century

67 Nos 41–5 High Street just missed being destroyed by the Great Fire which started close by. It expresses, better than any other house in the town, the typical medieval layout of a merchant's house. The hall, in the centre, is flanked by the projecting wings (of different dates) on either side. The lower framing of the left-hand wing and the upper framing of the centre has been replaced. One oddity is that the large curving braces on the ground floor were not 'answered'

68 Tinker's Hatch, in West Street, is a timber-framed late-medieval Wealden house – or rather, two-thirds of a Wealden house. The recessed hall in the centre and the right-hand wing, with its first floor jetty, still stand, but the matching left-hand wing has been demolished. It was probably built in the fifteenth century and the framing beneath the render is probably close-studded

69 No. 74 Smith Street is, despite appearances, another Wealden house, much remodelled. A floor has been inserted into the central hall and its front wall has been rebuilt in line with the upper storey of the flanking wings. In addition, the jetties of those wings have been underbuilt in stone

70 The Bowling Green in St Nicholas Church Street is another variation of the medieval hall house, built in the fifteenth century. In this case the differences between the different elements are less easy to detect at first glance. There are no jetties, for example. The two-bay hall in the middle was floored around 1600. To the left of the pub sign is the solar wing, with the service wing at the far right.

71 The Millwright's Arms in Coten End has a jettied first floor and dormer gables in the attic. The plain square framing and its original brick chimney suggest a date towards the end of the sixteenth century

10 Thomas Oken was a real benefactor to the less well-off in Warwick in the sixteenth century, and his house, in Castle Street, survived the Great Fire. Dating possibly to the late fifteenth or early sixteenth century, its most striking feature is the curved parallel braces in the jettied end gable. In the early nineteenth century, the dreaded School of Industry used part of the building, but now it has a much pleasanter role – as a doll museum

was usually flanked by a service wing at one end – the 'low' end – and a private wing for the owner, generally called the solar wing, at the 'high end'. In most examples, these two wings were structurally independent and usually of two storeys. Across the 'low' end of the hall was a cross, or 'screens', passage, reached by doors at either end.

Although no high status medieval houses survive in Warwick, some idea of the atmosphere of their halls can be gained in the Guild Hall and Priests Dining Room of Lord Leycester's Hospital – although these were not, of course, parts of houses. Several houses built for moderately wealthy medieval merchants and shopkeepers have survived and show the various ways in which the basic components of hall, service and solar could be arranged.

One of the oldest remnants of a medieval house is the fourteenth-century wing, with its original crown-post roof,

13 Now part of Lord Leycester's Hospital, this close-studded timber-framed building with the porch just inside the West Gate was built in the early sixteenth century. The porch itself is probably an early seventeenth-century addition. This was once the Anchor Inn

behind the oddly attractive Victorian mock-timber-framing of 37 Jury Street. A later, and more obvious example, is 41–5 High Street, opposite Lord Leycester's Hospital. Here the timber-framing to the street has been restored, and in part replaced, but the basic shape remains. A short and originally one-storey hall with a roof running parallel to the street is flanked by jettied two-storey cross-wings of different dates. The close-studded wing to the west is probably of the same date as the hall – the early fifteenth century – and was the solar. The other, with its braced gable end, was the service wing – probably rebuilt a century later. A floor was inserted into the hall to provide more accommodation in the sixteenth century, probably at the same time as a fireplace in a new chimney replaced the old open hearth. These were improvements seen in most houses of the period.

72 Largely due to the destruction wreaked by the Great Fire in the more prosperous centre of town, Warwick has few ornately framed 'half-timbered' buildings. The Tudor House Hotel in West Street was well away from the fire and escaped. It was built in the early seventeenth century, and has a different pattern of framing on each jettied floor. The bay furthest to the right was added slightly later and the cut-off 'dragon' beams can still be seen to show that the original right hand side wall was also jettied at each level

73 Brome House and Little Brome, in Bridge End, are parts of the same rather grand early seventeenth-century four-bay timber-framed house – one of the few of any pretensions in this now isolated and very peaceful suburb

The general arrangement of hall and flanking wings can be seen in several other houses in the town, but Warwick also has a few examples of an easily recognizable house type mainly seen in south-eastern England. The so-called 'Wealden' houses were built in their hundreds, particularly in Kent. For some unknown reason they were seldom built in large numbers elsewhere in England, but there are occasional isolated concentrations – and Warwickshire is the most significant of these, with examples in Coventry, Stratford-upon-Avon and Henley-in-Arden as well as in the county town itself. The Wealden is a compact structure that has all the main ingredients of a late-medieval house. The central open hall is, as usual, flanked by the solar and service wings. However, these are both jettied at first floor level and so their first floors project further forward than the wall of the hall. The hall and wings are covered by a single roof, and in between the wings the bottom of the roof slope is obviously some distance in front of the wall of the hall. It is supported by a timber known, dramatically, as a 'flying bressumer', between the wings, with curving braces at either end.

This type of house was particularly popular from the middle of the fifteenth century to the middle of the sixteenth century, and there is no reason to assume that the Warwick examples do not date from this period. The most obvious example of a Wealden is 105 West Street – Tinker's Hatch – although its northern wing is missing. It was clearly remodelled, extended, and a floor inserted in the hall – all work typical of the late sixteenth or early seventeenth century. Less obvious examples of Wealdens are at 74 Smith Street, and at least one, and possibly two, more in Mill Street.

Throughout the sixteenth century the grander medieval house gradually evolved into the type of house that we now consider to be normal, as privacy became more and more important. All the rooms were arranged on two or more floors, the better ones heated by fireplaces and lit by glazed windows. The communal life of the hall disappeared and individual rooms were assigned for individual uses – the previously separate kitchen became incorporated into the house; the parlour or withdrawing room replaced the hall as the place for

74 St John's House in Coten End was built on the site of a medieval hospital. The present house was started in about 1626 but the main block may have been the result of enlargement in the 1660s. This fine stone mansion, originally the home of the Stoughton family and later used as a school, is now a museum run by the County Council

75 The dramatic setting of Marble House's position, overlooking the Avon valley, has been badly affected by the later developments around it. The tall four-storey house is a fine example of mid-seventeenth-century work, with ogee-capped gables and a three-storey porch. The wings are later additions that detract from the sheer height of the original house

general socializing and relaxing; meals were taken in a separate dining room; and there were bedchambers and closets on the upper floors. The old hall got smaller and smaller until it was little more than the lobby it is now.

Despite the Great Fire, Warwick still has a few examples of the late sixteenth- and early seventeenth-century homes of its wealthier citizens, including the Tudor House on West Street, the Millwright's Arms in Coten End, and Brome House in Bridge End. Alongside these are more humble cottages of the same period, often just a single storey high with attics. All these are timber-framed, but at least three much more ambitious houses were built, in stone, on the outskirts of the town, and all three were still standing in the early years of this century. Now there are just two.

They were all built to a similar style and possibly all by the same unknown master mason. The best preserved is

in Coten End, and part of the County Museum – St John's House, built on the site of the twelfth-century St John's Hospital. The present building was started in about 1626 by Anthony Stoughton but radically remodelled in the 1660s. The structural evidence seems to point to the two rear wings – slightly lower and with slightly rougher ashlar – being part of the original house. The impressive frontage block was probably part of the later rebuilding – carried out in the same general style. Both elements have the distinctive 'ogee' type gables and ornately moulded string courses. By the end of the eighteenth century the house was used as a private school and in 1830 was described as an 'academy for young ladies'. At the start of the twentieth century it was used as a records office for the Army, and was bought by the county council in 1960. It opened as a museum in the following year – and is well worth a visit.

76 On the hopper head of this house in Smith Street, not far beyond the East Gate, are the initials 'P.C.' and the date 1686. These presumably date to the addition of the stone bay to the slightly earlier timber-framed bays next to it – although the hopper itself must surely not be in its original position

Warwickshire still, as yet, has admirably resisted the economic pressures to start charging people to view their own heritage.

At the opposite end of the town, commanding fine views over the racecourse, is Marble House – not its original name but one given to it later because of its proximity to the Smith's building yard in the early eighteenth century. Unlike the long, low design of St John's House, it takes full advantage of its position. The original portion is a four-storey tower, just three bays wide with a projecting three-storey porch. Nevertheless, it shares the same ashlar stonework, string courses, and ogee gables, and was probably built in the early to mid-seventeenth century. The two low battlemented wings were added in 1812, when the house was owned by William Parkes, and most of the original stone mullioned and transommed windows were

23 Landor House, just outside the East Gate in Smith Street, was built by Roger Hurlbut in 1692, just before the Great Fire. It provided a good example for those rebuilding the town afterwards to copy. The poet Walter Savage Landor was born here in 1775 and a few years after the Girls High School took over the house in 1879 they gave it its present name in his honour

probably replaced by sashes at the same period. Today the house is rather hemmed in by the later developments all around it – mainly started by Parkes himself at the beginning of the nineteenth century and continuing until the present. Despite this, the views over the Avon valley from the upper floors must still be quite splendid.

The third house of this trio was, like St John's House, built on the site of a former religious foundation, in this case, the early twelfth-century Augustinian Priory of St Sepulchre. Originally built in 1566, The Priory was remodelled in about 1620 and may have been the prototype for the other two. By the nineteenth century it was in a poor state and by the 1920s was empty and threatened with demolition. No one came forward with any positive ways to save it and it was eventually bought by an American diplomat, A.W. Weddell, and dismantled stone by stone. He shipped the pieces across

77 Mill Street escaped the Great Fire, so it is difficult to know whether No. 12, which looks to date from ten years or so either side of 1700, was built before or after it. An earlier date might be suggested by the use of cross-mullioned casement windows rather than sashes, but in most respects the design is very similar to the post-fire rebuilding

78 No. 23 High Street is a fine example of a post-1694 building, in brick with stone quoins, string course, and keystones. Although it is close to the centre of the town, it is still seven bays wide. On the side wall are typical blind windows to complete the architectural design, and a huge full-height window to light the stairs

78 In Warwick as elsewhere, it was quite usual only to worry about the design of the front of the houses and the backs could be fairly haphazard. The back of 23 High Street is better than most, but still has none of the symmetry of the front. The Gothick tracery in the sashes is probably the result of a later remodelling

79 Aylesford House is on the corner of High Street and Castle Street, right in the centre of old Warwick and by the site of the old Cross. After the 1694 fire, the three houses on this central crossroads (the fourth corner being taken up by the Court House) were designed to be relatively grand affairs. Despite its white paint, this is one of the finest late seventeenth-century townhouses in the region.

the Atlantic to Richmond, Virginia, and re-used many of them in his new mansion, Virginia House. Part of the old service quarter is now occupied by the County Records Office.

Even before the Great Fire, the general pattern of the better class houses of late seventeenth-and early eighteenth-century Warwick had been set by Landor House, built just outside the East Gate by Roger Hurlbutt in 1692. The fire simply hurried the process of rebuilding dramatically, giving central Warwick its unique place in English urban architectural history. Well balanced and elegant, and, like most of the houses built before it, Landor House was built along the street rather than end on to it, and other architects and builders clearly copied its general principle in the great rebuilding. Some of the new houses were built as single large houses, others built as extremely grand semi-detached

27 Another pair of houses designed to look like one larger one is 18–20 Northgate Street. Built just after the fire in brick with stone dressings, the slightly projecting pedimented centre has a larger window representing the door of the supposed mansion, flanked by the real doors to the two houses in the normal position of windows. It is such a shame that it has been painted pale grey – and that the two owners couldn't agree on how to mend the oval window in the pediment.

80 The Mill House, south of the river in Bridge End, is a late seventeenth-century brick building that has retained many of its original features, including its cross-mullioned casements with their rectangular leaded glazing. The porch is not part of the original design

28 The closely set cross-mullioned casement windows and general proportions of 24 Castle Street all seem to point to a late seventeenth-century date, or certainly one very early in the eighteenth century. However, recent documentary research indicates it was built around 1750 – an example of rather backward provincial architecture. It became two houses in the nineteenth century

9 No. 3 New Street, with is bay windows, first floor niche, and half-round, or 'lunette' window, is a rather busy mid-eighteenth-century design not copied elsewhere in the town

81 No. 10 Church Street, now the Athenaeum, is a remarkably sophisticated mid- to-late eighteenth-century house for Warwick, with its elegant pedimented centre-piece, full-height ground floor rustication, and Corinthian pilasters. It became a country club in the nineteenth century. Despite some repairs to the façade, it has suffered little alteration since it was built

82 This section of the Lord Leycester Hotel in Jury Street was built in the late eighteenth century and is a good example of its period – well-cared for and little altered. The five-bay design is not quite symmetrical, the right-hand bay containing the driveway through to the yard being slightly recessed

83 This isolated late eighteenth-century house is in Theatre Street and still retains most of its main features intact – despite obvious damage to the fine 'rubbed' bricks in the flat-arched window heads. The door has a delicate 'Adamesque' fanlight above it and the thin glazing bars of the deeply recessed sashes are typical of its date

84 Blackfriars House, just outside the West Gate, is an elegant though rather grave neo-classical late-Georgian design faced with good quality ashlar

85 In order to provide an official residence for the travelling judges presiding at the courts in the Shire Hall, this house was finished in 1816 alongside it. The design is simple, with horizontal rustication of the ground floor, a tall first floor, and a Greek Ionic porch. The architect was Henry Hakewill and it cost the then remarkably high figure of £8,000

ones, made to look like larger ones. This peculiarly English house-type remains the most common form today – but there is a world of difference between Warwick's late-1690s Northgate House, surely one of the best 'semis' in the land, and the average little brick-and-breeze-block boxes built in their hundreds of thousands this century.

Apart from the piecemeal replacement of houses in the centre, little else has really changed since. Attempts to create grand suburbs in the late eighteenth century came to nothing, with only a few tall Georgian houses built. Later, the influence of Leamington Spa, fashionable in the early Victorian period, made its presence felt in some rather bizarre terraces on the east side of town and the occasional stuccoed villa. Later still came the typical leafy middle-class suburban streets and the less leafy streets of two-storey semi-detached and terraced brick houses for the artisans. Virtually all these houses are built

86 While the semi-detached house was always popular in eighteenth-century Warwick, the grand terraces fashionable elsewhere were not. This late-eighteenth-century row in the Butts is one of the very few examples, built of brick but faced in ashlar

87 The Dolls House in St Nicholas Church Street was built in the early nineteenth century to house the curate of the nearby church – suitably close to the Vicarage nearby. The Gothic style used is somewhat odd – neither playful nor serious

88 Improvements in transport allowed the use of building materials brought in from elsewhere in the country – like the dark grey brick facing this astonishing row of large mid-Victorian houses in Coten End. The style is vaguely neo-Tudor

89 The Gothic Revival even affected this pair of early twentieth-century 'semis' in Albert Street. They are otherwise typical of buildings put up in their hundreds of thousands from the late nineteenth century onwards

111

to basic patterns, but monotony is relieved by often quite entertaining, if occasionally somewhat peculiar, architectural conceits and motifs.

The twentieth-century houses of Warwick are neither better nor worse than those of any other similar Midland town, and it has been spared the high rise – the nearest to it being the modern, plain, but generously spaced estate of flats and maisonettes at the back of St John's House.

90 These modern flats close to Coten End are pleasant enough without trying to achieve much in the way of architectural effect. At least the setting is well cared for. Perhaps in fifty or a hundred years' time architectural critics will actually like them and howl if anyone plans to knock them down

Industrial
Buildings

Warwick has never been an important industrial town, despite attempts to make it so. It has always suffered from poor transport links with the rest of the Midlands, despite its position at a natural river crossing. There were plans to improve things from the medieval period onwards and, according to one source, as early as the start of the fifteenth century the then Earl of Warwick planned to make the 'plesont syght of the vessels comyng and a makyng to Warrewik' on the Avon a reality. Nothing came of those plans, and in the seventeenth century the river was only made navigable as far upstream as Stratford-upon-Avon. The town had to rely on the invariably unreliable road system until the very start of the nineteenth century.

Roads from the south converged on the old medieval bridge. The first mention of a bridge at Warwick, in 1208, probably indicates that there was already one across the river by the twelfth century. This medieval bridge was probably of timber, supported by stone piers, and by the late fourteenth century was in a state of disrepair. It was then completely rebuilt in stone and took all the traffic over the Avon for the next four hundred years. With the increases in road traffic and the improvements in the roads themselves, the bridge was getting to be a bit of a bottleneck by the later eighteenth century, and in constant need of repair. The need for, and the cost of, a new bridge was an important factor in the Earl of Warwick's negotiations with the townsfolk in his attempts to extend the castle grounds and get rid of the main road from the bridge passing right beneath his castle walls.

91 The single graceful arch of the New, or Great, Bridge was built a few hundred yards upstream from the ancient medieval structure mainly at the expense of the owner of the castle who was anxious to extend his grounds and privacy. It was designed by William Eborall and opened in 1793, after his death

With the Earl promising to pay for most of the costs of a new bridge himself, the citizens were persuaded to divert the Banbury road to the east to approach a new crossing several hundred yards upstream from the old. The graceful single 105 foot long arch of this new structure – the Great Bridge – was designed by William Eborall of Warwick, who died before his great work was finished. It was built of stone shipped by boat from Emscote, cost about £4,000 – of which the Earl paid all but £1,000 – and opened in 1793. Much of the old bridge was finally swept away by floods soon afterwards, leaving a few overgrown, and suitably Romantic, ruined arches that can be best admired from the castle battlements.

The dawning of the Canal Age briefly brought new hope to Warwick's traders in the last years of the eighteenth century. Waterways built by two completely separate undertakings met at Saltisford. The Warwick & Birmingham and the Warwick &

93 This timeless canal scene could be in the heart of the countryside. Instead, it is on the outskirts of Warwick on the former Warwick & Napton Canal not far from the Avon aqueduct

Napton canals both opened in early 1800, but were never particularly successful. After decades of struggle, both eventually became part of the new Grand Union system in 1929. The canals are still in use, for leisure now rather than for trade, and the tow-path walks give a very different perspective of Warwick. The only major engineering work in the town connected with the canals is the Avon Aqueduct, taking the former Warwick & Napton line over the river. The aqueduct is a three-arched stone-faced structure, probably designed jointly by the canal's engineer, Charles Handley, and a member of its Committee, Henry Couchman. The upstream view is slightly marred by a modern parapet, but the downstream view is much better. New metal steps on the steep-sided embankment provide a useful link between the canal tow-path walk and the riverside footpath linking Warwick and Leamington Spa – a very welcome idea.

The arrival of the canals led to serious attempts to establish manufacturing industries in the town – spinning, linen and lace – but within a few decades it was reported that 'the cotton manufacture . . . has entirely declined, and a worsted manufactury is decreasing . . .'. By the 1970s there were still a few architectural reminders of these industries. Now there are virtually none.

Warwick can still boast one of the most important industrial buildings in the country, however, and one that was served by the canal basin in Saltisford. The development of gas lighting in the early nineteenth century revolutionized the way towns looked at night. The former gasworks in Saltisford was built in 1822. The new technology, as is so often, and not unreasonably, the case, was distrusted and steps had to be taken to alleviate any potential danger. When coal gas was made, it was stored in gasholders, a type of structure that later

94 Historic Warwick is not, perhaps, the place where one would expect to find one of the oldest and best preserved gasworks in the world! The works were opened next to the Saltisford canal basin in 1822 and the frontage block, flanked by the gasholders, was designed to look like anything but a gasworks, with its Gothick windows and stuccoed façade

became a well-known landmark of any town and was usually referred to – wrongly – as a gasometer. The gasholders of the Warwick site were housed in octagonal brick towers at either end of the office range. The whole stuccoed frontage was given a degree of elegance with round-headed windows and Gothick glazing bars – those in the corner towers being, of course, false. Although most of the original buildings behind the frontage have long gone, the rest has been tastefully converted to office use.

Warwick also has the remains of a building connected with the early years of another major energy source – electricity. There has been a mill at Warwick on the weir by the castle since time immemorial – it was, after all, an ideal natural site for one. The present mill was rebuilt by Thomas Lightoler in 1768 in a Gothick style using stone from Emscote. The design, obviously, was deliberately chosen to fit in with the castle that

95 There has probably been a mill on the site of the Castle Mill, served by the natural weir across the Avon, since Saxon times. The present Gothick building of 1768 is by Thomas Lightoler, but was gutted in 1880. It then became an electricity generator, serving the castle and remained operable until the mid-twentieth century

towers above it. The mill was gutted by fire in 1880 but reopened in 1894 as an electricity generator to provide the castle with what was then an exciting new form of lighting. It only ceased to be used for this purpose after the Second World War.

Index

Page numbers in bold indicate illustrations.